Eyewitness
CHRISTIANITY

Russian Orthodox icons

Salvation Army song leader playing a cornet

Holy water stoup

Stained glass fragment depicting the Madonna and Child

Horn of Saint Hubert

Abbot's crozier

Model of the *Mayflower*

Eyewitness
CHRISTIANITY

Written by
PHILIP WILKINSON

Photographed by
STEVE TEAGUE

Illuminated Latin psalter

DK Publishing, Inc.

Carving of
an angel
swinging
a censer

Gargoyle

Censer and
incense
boat on
stand

Statue of
Saint Joseph

LONDON, NEW YORK, MUNICH,
MELBOURNE, AND DELHI

For Bookwork Ltd.
Editor Annabel Blackledge
Art editor Kate Mullins

For DK Publishing
Managing editor
Andrew Macintyre
Managing art editors
Clare Shedden, Jane Thomas
U.S. editors Margaret Parrish, Christine Heilman
Category publisher Linda Martin
Production controller Erica Rosen
Picture researchers
Angela Anderson, Bridget Tily
Picture librarian Claire Bowers
DTP designer Siu Yin Ho
Jacket Designer Dean Price

Consultants
Annette Reynolds,
AD Publishing Services Ltd.,
Jon Reynolds, Diocesan Director of Education

REVISED EDITION
Editor John Searcy
Writer Elizabeth Hester
Consultant Peggy Morgan
Publishing director Beth Sutinis
Senior designer Tai Blanche
Designer Diana Catherines
Photo research Chrissy McIntyre
Art director Dirk Kaufman
DTP designer Kathy Farias
Production Ivor Parker

This edition published in the United States in 2006 by
DK Publishing, Inc.
375 Hudson Street
New York, New York 10014

06 07 08 09 10 10 9 8 7 6 5 4 3 2 1

A catalog record for this book
is available from the Library of Congress.

ISBN-10 0-7566-2246-8
ISBN-13 978-0-7566-2246-6 (HC)

ISBN-10 0-7566-2247-6 -
ISBN-13 978-0-7566-2247-3 (ALB)

Color reproduction by
Colourscan, Singapore
Printed in Hong Kong by Toppan
Printing Co., (Shenzen) Ltd.

Discover more at

www.dk.com

Bread and wine for
Holy Communion

Rosary
with medals

Rosary
medal

Model of
a baroque
church

Contents

Abbot in ceremonial robes

In the beginning

THE BIBLE BEGINS WITH stories of the creation of the world and the early Jewish people. These books, which make up the Old Testament of the Christian Bible, and which are also sacred to the Jews, were written by Jewish scribes long before the birth of Jesus. For the Jews they are important because they describe the covenant, or special relationship, between God and the Jewish people. For Christians the Old Testament has added significance because many of the stories seem to prefigure, or mirror, events that happened later when Jesus came to save humankind from sin.

Fourth-century depiction of Adam and Eve in Eden

FORBIDDEN FRUIT
Genesis, the first book of the Bible (p. 20), tells how God created Heaven and Earth, land and water, animals and birds, and finally Adam and Eve—the first man and woman. God put them in the Garden of Eden, and told them that the only fruit they must not eat was the fruit of the Tree of Knowledge.

ENEMY IN EDEN
Satan, who lived in Hell (pp. 26–27), was God's archenemy. Early Jewish writers said that the serpent in the Garden of Eden, a cunning tempter, was Satan in disguise. In the Book of Genesis, the serpent tempts Eve to eat the forbidden fruit, just as Satan later tempted Jesus in the New Testament.

The serpent is often pictured as a snake like this red spitting cobra

The forbidden fruit is often imagined to have been an apple

ORIGINAL SIN
The serpent tempted Eve to eat the forbidden fruit, and Adam followed suit. God was angry at their disobedience and threw them out of the Garden of Eden. Christians believe that Adam and Eve, and their descendants, were tainted with this "original sin." Only the coming of Jesus Christ would eventually offer humankind a way of escaping sin and achieving everlasting life with God.

This 12th-century painting of Satan shows him with Saint Michael

Saint Michael is weighing souls to determine whether they should go to Heaven or Hell

Satan

The dove brought Noah a leaf to show that the flood waters were going down

THE GREAT FLOOD
Another story in Genesis tells how God became disenchanted with all the evil in the world, and sent a great flood to destroy much of the wickedness. Only one good man, Noah, was allowed to escape with his family. He built a great boat, the ark, in which he, his sons and their wives, and all the birds and animals took refuge. Christians think of Noah as the second father of the human race, after Adam.

Mosaic of Noah and his family in the ark

> *"Do not lay a hand on the boy, he said. Do not do anything to him. Now I know that you fear God."*
>
> **GENESIS 22:12**
> Angel of the Lord to Abraham

God provided a ram for Abraham's sacrifice

SACRIFICIAL RAM
God ordered Abraham to kill his son Isaac as a sacrifice. Abraham was about to obey when an angel told him to stop and kill a ram instead. Christians see this story as a prophecy of the way in which God would sacrifice Jesus.

Daniel window from Augsburg Cathedral in Germany

Isaiah window from Augsburg Cathedral in Germany

Moses window from Augsburg Cathedral in Germany

PROPHETS AND LEADERS
The Old Testament contains stories about Jewish ancestors such as Abraham and the great leader Moses, who guided the Jews from slavery in Egypt back to their homeland. The Old Testament also includes writings about and by prophets such as Isaiah and Daniel, who told of the coming of a Messiah, or savior.

The birth of Jesus

THE GOSPELS (p. 21) tell how a virgin called Mary gave birth to Jesus Christ in Bethlehem. Followers of Christ (Christians) believe that Jesus was God's son, and that the prophets of the Old Testament had predicted he would come and save humankind from sin. The idea that God became human in this way is called the incarnation, meaning that God's spirit was made into human flesh. The birth of Jesus marked the origin of the Christian religion.

HUMBLE BEGINNINGS
Mary and Joseph were staying in Bethlehem at the time of the nativity, or birth, of Jesus. All the inns in the town were full, so Jesus had to be born in the humblest of surroundings—a stable.

The angels play instruments that were popular in the 16th century, when this altarpiece was made

Mary is traditionally shown wearing blue

MADONNA AND CHILD
Statues of Mary, or the Madonna, and the infant Jesus are a reminder of Mary's vital role in the Christian story. She is a link between the human and spiritual worlds.

The Holy Spirit is shown in the form of a dove

Modern mosaic from Old Plaza Church in California

THE ANNUNCIATION
Luke's Gospel describes how the angel Gabriel appeared to Mary to tell her that, even though she was a virgin, she was about to become pregnant. Gabriel announced that Mary would be visited by the Holy Spirit (p. 26) and would give birth to God's son, who would be a king whose rule would last forever. Mary was told to call her son Jesus.

John carries a banner bearing Latin words meaning "Behold the Lamb of God"

John wears camel-hair clothes, the typical garments of a prophet

JOHN THE BAPTIST
John led the life of a prophet and preacher, encouraging people to repent their sins and be baptized. John's preaching prepared the way for Jesus, and when Jesus grew up he asked John to baptize him in the Jordan River.

Statue by Donatello, 1386–1466

GLAD TIDINGS
Luke's account of the nativity describes how angels appeared to shepherds in the fields just outside Bethlehem. The angels told them the good news of Jesus' birth and the shepherds came down from the fields into the town to worship the newborn king. This story shows that Jesus is important to everyone, even "outsiders" like the shepherds.

HOC·OPVS·FECIT· FIERI PHILIPPVS· THOME PHILIPPI· DE PANICHISANO DNI ·M·D·X X I·

God looks down from Heaven

FOLLOW THE STAR
Matthew's Gospel tells how the Magi, or wise men, followed a star from the east to Jerusalem in search of a child born to rule the people of Israel. King Herod sent them to Bethlehem, where they found Jesus.

14th-century pendant showing the Magi and Jesus

Gold

Frankincense

Myrrh

FIT FOR A KING
The Magi worshipped Jesus and gave him three gifts: gold, frankincense, and myrrh. The symbolism of these gifts may be interpreted in different ways. One interpretation is that gold represents riches, frankincense kingship, and myrrh a special spiritual calling.

The shepherds watch their flocks of sheep

15th-century stained glass from Ulm Cathedral in Germany

ROYAL RIVALRY
King Herod ruled the Holy Land on behalf of the Romans. According to Matthew, he tried to destroy Jesus, whom he saw as a rival to his throne. Herod told his men to kill all the children in Bethlehem who were less than two years old. God warned Joseph of this, and he escaped with Mary and Jesus to Egypt.

Mary, her husband Joseph, and the baby Jesus

Glazed earthenware altarpiece made by Giovanni della Robbia, 1521

Parables and lessons

Jesus' favorite way of teaching was to use parables—short stories that make their point by means of a simple comparison. Jesus used these parables to talk about the kingdom of God, and to illustrate how people should behave toward each other. Jesus also preached moral lectures called sermons. The most famous of these was the Sermon on the Mount, in which he explained the key features of the kingdom of God (p. 26) and the Christian way of life. Above all, Jesus said that you should "Do for others what you want them to do for you."

THE LOST SON
This parable tells of a man who divided his wealth between his two sons. The younger son went off and spent his share, while his brother worked hard at home. When the younger son returned, his father killed his prize calf for a celebratory feast. The elder son objected, but his father said, "He was lost, but now he has been found." These Chinese illustrations show the story from the handing over of the money to the family feast.

SERMON ON THE MOUNT
In this sermon Jesus said that members of God's kingdom should try to achieve the perfection shown by God. For example, he explained that it is not enough simply to obey the commandment, "Do not commit murder." Christians should avoid anger completely.

The disciples have haloes, to indicate their holiness

19th-century window of the Good Samaritan

THE GOOD SAMARITAN
Jesus taught that you should love your neighbor. When someone asked Jesus, "Who is my neighbor?" he told this story: A man was robbed and left for dead. A Jewish priest and a Levite passed, but did not help. Then a Samaritan—a member of a group scorned by the Jews—came by. He helped the injured man and took him to safety. The Samaritan was the true neighbor.

PLANTING WORDS
Jesus compared his words to seeds scattered by a farmer. Some of the seed fell on the path and was stepped on. Some fell on rocky ground or among thorn bushes, where seedlings could not grow. Finally, some fell on good soil and grew into corn. Jesus said that people who heard and understood his words were like the good soil.

Sower's bag and seeds

LESSON OF THE FIG TREE
Jesus told people to think of a fig tree. When its leaves start to appear, people know that summer is on its way. Similarly, they should look out for signs of Jesus' second coming. When strange things happen to the moon and stars, when whole countries are in despair, and people are faint from fear, then they will know that the kingdom of God is about to come.

Figs and fig leaf

Jesus would probably have sat down to deliver the sermon

THE LORD'S PRAYER

Jesus gave his most important lesson about prayer in the Sermon on the Mount. He told his listeners not to pray ostentatiously with long, elaborate prayers—God knows what you need before you ask. Instead, he gave them the *Lord's Prayer* beginning, "Our Father in Heaven, hallowed be your name…". It has been translated into languages as diverse as Spanish and Chinese, and is repeated in Christian churches the world over.

Pater noster qui es in caelis ⁑ Sanctificetur nomen tuum ⁑ Adveniat regnum tuum ⁑ Fiat voluntas tuas sicut in caelo et in terra ⁑ Panem nostrum quotidianum da nobis hodie ⁑ Et dimitte nobis debita nostra sicut et nos dimittimus debitoribus nostris ⁑ Et ne nos inducas in temptatione ⁑ Sed libera nos a malo ⁑ Amen ⁑

Horn book with the text of the *Lord's Prayer* in Latin

15th-century fresco by Fra Angelico

Common poppies

"Blessed are the merciful, for they will be shown mercy. Blessed are the pure in heart, for they will see God."

MATTHEW 5:7–8
Jesus' Sermon on the Mount

FLOWERY FINERY

During the Sermon on the Mount, Jesus told his listeners that they should not care too much about everyday things like food and clothes. Wild flowers do not have fine garments, but they are still beautifully dressed. People should be concerned with God's kingdom, not with possessions or finery.

The Crucifixion

Jesus warned his disciples several times that he would soon die. He told them that the Jewish chief priests would reject him, that he would be killed, and that he would rise again after three days. The disciples failed to understand these warnings, and were unprepared for what happened when Jesus went to Jerusalem. Jesus was put on trial and condemned to death on the cross. This is the most solemn part of the Christian story, but it is also the major turning point—Christians believe Jesus' blood was spilled so that they could be granted eternal life with God.

ENTRY INTO JERUSALEM
Jesus rode into Jerusalem on a donkey, as shown in this painting from the Oratory of Saint Pellegrino in Italy. Many people laid down palm leaves, or even their coats, to cover the dusty path in front of him. They were happy because the prophet Zechariah had predicted that their king would arrive on a donkey.

Christ looks triumphant, not suffering

ON THE CROSS
In Jesus' time crucifixion was the normal way in which the Romans imposed the death sentence. Jesus was crucified between two criminals, and the Gospels recall that his death took about three hours—much faster than usual. At the point of Jesus' death the curtain in the Temple in Jerusalem was torn in two and an earthquake shook the ground.

BODY AND BLOOD
At the Last Supper with his disciples, Jesus broke the bread and told them to eat it, saying, "This is my body." He then gave them the wine, saying, "This is my blood." When Christians celebrate Communion (pp. 52–53) they remember or recreate these events.

10th-century crucifix from Denmark, made of gilded carved oak

Jesus is shown with the marks of the nails in his palms

Rosary medal showing Jesus carrying his cross

A modern reconstruction of the crown of thorns

Rosary medal showing Jesus wearing the crown of thorns

THE ROAD TO CALVARY
Jesus was flogged and mocked before his death. Because he had been called King of the Jews he was forced to wear a crown of thorns. He was made to carry his heavy cross along the steep road to Calvary, the place of crucifixion. Jesus tried but he was too weak, so a spectator, Simon of Cyrene, carried it for him.

A CONDEMNED MAN
The council elders took Jesus to Pontius Pilate, the Roman governor, who had the power to impose the death penalty. Jesus was accused of setting himself up as King of the Jews but, when asked about this, Jesus simply said, "So you say." Pilate was unwilling to condemn Jesus, and said the crowd could choose one prisoner to be set free. But they refused to release Jesus.

IN DENIAL
Jesus was taken to the High Priest, Caiaphas, and was put before the supreme Jewish council. As the disciple Peter sat outside he was accused three times of being one of Jesus' followers, but he denied it each time. A rooster crowed as Peter made his third denial. Jesus had told Peter that this would happen.

Many churches have a rooster weather vane to remind us of the denial

THE LAST SUPPER
At the time of Jesus' arrest it was Passover—the festival that celebrates the freeing of the Jews from slavery and looks forward to the coming of the Messiah. Jesus told his disciples to arrange a Passover meal. He said that this would be the last meal he would share with them and that one of them would soon betray him.

13th-century Syriac manuscript

The Kiss of Judas by Giotto di Bondone

JUDAS KISS
After the Last Supper, Jesus went to the Garden of Gethsemane. His disciple Judas Iscariot arrived with Roman soldiers and the Jewish Temple guard. Judas greeted Jesus with a kiss—a signal he had arranged with the soldiers. The soldiers arrested Jesus, who told his disciples not to resist but to accept God's will.

The Resurrection

CHRISTIANS BELIEVE that on the third day after his crucifixion Jesus rose from the dead. The Gospels (p. 21) describe how, when he appeared to his disciples after the Resurrection, some of them did not recognize him. Jesus' body seemed to have changed, and he apparently was able to appear and disappear at will. Christians believe in the Resurrection in different ways. Some are convinced that the risen Jesus was literally alive on Earth. Others believe his presence was a spiritual one, seen only in the ways in which his followers behaved. Most Christians believe that Jesus joined God in Heaven, where he will stay until the Last Judgment (p. 26).

STRONG SYMBOL
The Resurrection is one of the most important parts of the Christian story. It is often depicted symbolically, as in the case of this embroidered decoration from a priest's clothing.

John, whose symbol is an eagle

Matthew, whose symbol is a man

THE EMPTY CROSS
An empty cross is a reminder of Jesus' resurrection. The lamb at the center is a familiar symbol of Jesus, who is often referred to as the Lamb of God. The lamb is an innocent creature that is easily killed, so it reminds Christians of the sacrifice made by God in order to redeem humankind from sin.

Mark, whose symbol is a lion

ROCK TOMB
Joseph of Arimathea, a disciple of Jesus, offered his own tomb for Jesus' burial. This tomb was probably similar to the one above. Called an arcosolium, it has been cut into the rock of a cliff face and sealed with a large, round stone.

RISEN FROM THE DEAD
Pontius Pilate ordered soldiers to guard Jesus' tomb in case the disciples came to take away his body. But the Gospels tell how, on the third day after the Crucifixion, Jesus rose from the dead while the guards slept. This set of three 15th-century Italian paintings (see also opposite) shows Jesus rising from a Roman-style sarcophagus, or tomb, set into the rocks.

SUPPER AT EMMAUS

Shortly after the Resurrection, Jesus met two of his disciples near a village called Emmaus. The pair did not recognize him, but invited him to supper with some other disciples. It was only when Jesus broke the bread and blessed it that they recognized him. Then he disappeared from their sight.

Illustration from a 15th-century Italian Bible

DOUBTING THOMAS

The disciple Thomas said that he would believe in Jesus' resurrection only if he saw the wounds that Jesus had received when he was crucified. John's Gospel recalls that, when Jesus met the disciples, he showed Thomas his wounds.

Mural from the Holy Trinity Church in Sopocani, Serbia, c. 1265

Jesus is shown surrounded by clouds and angels

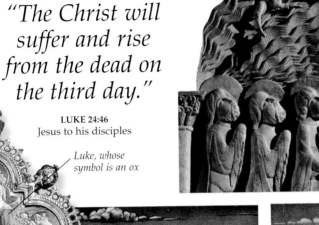

THE ASCENSION

The Gospels and another New Testament book called Acts record that, after telling his disciples to spread the word (pp. 18–19), Jesus joined his Father in Heaven. He was raised up into the sky and then vanished behind a cloud.

12th-century stone relief from Saint Dominic's Abbey in Silos, Spain

> *"The Christ will suffer and rise from the dead on the third day."*
>
> LUKE 24:46
> Jesus to his disciples

Luke, whose symbol is an ox

THE EMPTY TOMB

A group of women, probably including Jesus' follower Mary Magdalene, went to the tomb to anoint his body with spices. When they arrived, they found the tomb open and empty. An angel appeared to them and told them that Jesus had risen from the dead. In Matthew's account of this story, the amazing news was accompanied by an earthquake.

LOOKING FOR JESUS

John's Gospel contains a moving account of Mary Magdalene's search for Jesus' body. As she wept at his disappearance, a man appeared whom Mary believed to be a gardener. But when he spoke her name, she realized immediately that it was Jesus. He said, "Do not hold on to me, because I have not yet gone back up to the Father."

The Bible was actually written by many different people. The books of the Old Testament were written by unknown scribes over hundreds of years. The authors of the New Testament were early Christians. Scribes later made copies of these original texts by hand using quill pens.

Quill pens and ink horns

God's book

T HE CHRISTIAN BIBLE consists of more than 60 separate books written over many centuries. These books are divided into two main groups. The Old Testament contains the history and sacred writings of the Jewish people before the time of Jesus, which are sacred to Jews as well as to Christians. The New Testament deals mainly with Jesus and his early followers. The original texts (the Old Testament written in Hebrew and Aramaic, and the New in Greek) were translated into modern languages by biblical scholars in the 20th century (pp. 34–35).

Mosaic of the creation of the birds, Monreale Cathedral, Sicily

THE FIRST FIVE
The first five books of the Bible describe the creation of the universe and tell stories of the earliest Jewish ancestors. One of the most important stories relates how Moses received the Tablets of Law, or Ten Commandments, from God. It is sometimes claimed that Moses was the author of these books.

GETTING HISTORICAL
Many of the Old Testament books are historical, following the fate of the Jewish people over hundreds of years. These historical writings describe events in the lives of notable kings, such as Solomon, who was famously visited from afar by the Queen of Sheba and her entourage.

HOLY PLACE
Built by King Solomon, the Temple in Jerusalem was the holiest of all places to the Jews. It was destroyed by the Babylonians, but the Jews eventually restored it. In the Roman period, the Temple was rebuilt again by Herod the Great. Luke's Gospel describes Jesus visiting this temple as a boy.

Artist's impression of Solomon's Temple in the time of Christ

2,500-year-old carved head of a woman from Sheba

13th-century illustration of David playing a harp

THE WORDS OF THE PROPHETS
A large number of Old Testament books contain the sayings of prophets, such as Jeremiah, Isaiah, and Ezekiel. These men brought messages from God, telling people about God's will in relation to everything from everyday life to the future of the Jewish people. To early Christians, many of the prophets' words seemed to predict the coming of Jesus.

Depiction of Jeremiah from a 12th-century wall painting from Cyprus

Illustration of Paul's death from a 12th-century manuscript

WORDS OF WISDOM
The wisdom books are a group of Old Testament books written in various styles and on a range of subjects. The Psalms (originally said to have been written by King David) contain poetry praising God; the Proverbs consist of pithy, instructive sayings; and other books, such as Job, discuss human suffering.

13th-century illustration of Jonah and the fish

STORY WITH A MORAL
God told the prophet Jonah to visit the city of Nineveh to persuade the people to repent their sins. When Jonah refused, God sent a storm. Jonah was thrown overboard from his ship, and was swallowed by a great fish. When the fish finally spewed Jonah onto dry land, the prophet went straight to Nineveh.

WORK OF GOD
The later books of the New Testament are concerned mostly with the work of Jesus' followers, who carried on his mission after the Resurrection. This work is described both in the book of Acts and in the various epistles (letters) written by early church leaders such as Saint Paul.

SEEING TOGETHER
The first four books of the New Testament—the Gospels— tell the story of Jesus' life, crucifixion, and resurrection. The Gospels of Matthew, Mark, and Luke are very similar and are known as the "synoptic" (seeing together) Gospels. These were probably written soon after A.D. 65. John's Gospel is thought to have been written at the end of the first century.

Luke, the winged ox

The symbols of the evangelists, or writers of the Gospels, by modern artist Laura James

John, the eagle

Matthew, the angel

Mark, the lion

Continued on next page

Early Bible texts

The books of the Bible were first written down by hand in the local languages of the eastern Mediterranean—Hebrew, Aramaic, and Greek. When different scribes copied out the texts, small variations occurred. The books were then translated into other ancient languages, such as Syriac. As a result, scholars translating the Bible into modern languages have a range of different sources to refer to, which helps them to make their version as close as possible to the original.

GUIDANCE FROM GOD

The Hebrew Bible—the Torah plus other books of narrative, prophecy, and wisdom—also makes up the Old Testament of the Christian Bible. Jesus often referred to these ancient Jewish scriptures, calling them the Law or the Writings. The five books that make up the Torah are Genesis, Exodus, Leviticus, Numbers, and Deuteronomy. They are central to the Jewish faith, and Deuteronomy includes 613 commandments that Jews try to follow in their everyday lives.

Crownlike finials, or tips, indicate the importance of the Torah

Tik, or Torah case, used by Spanish, Middle Eastern, and North African Jews

COVER UP

In the west, the Torah is usually kept in a cloth covering called a mantle. This is often embroidered with religious symbols. On this mantle, the crown is the symbol of the Torah, the Hebrew writing reads "Crown of the Torah," and the lions represent Judah, one of the tribes of Israel.

EARLIEST EXAMPLES

The Dead Sea Scrolls were found at Qumran in Jordan, on the edge of the Dead Sea, in 1947. They contain the earliest surviving manuscripts of most of the books of the Old Testament and also other texts in Hebrew, Greek, and Aramaic written down as early as the second century B.C.

Pottery scroll jars

HIDDEN TREASURE

The original owners of the Dead Sea Scrolls were members of a Jewish group called the Essenes. They kept the texts in large pottery jars. When their area was overrun by the Romans, the Essenes hid the Scrolls, which lay undiscovered for almost 2,000 years. Most of the Scrolls were damaged, but they have helped modern Bible translators, and taught scholars much about life in the first century A.D.

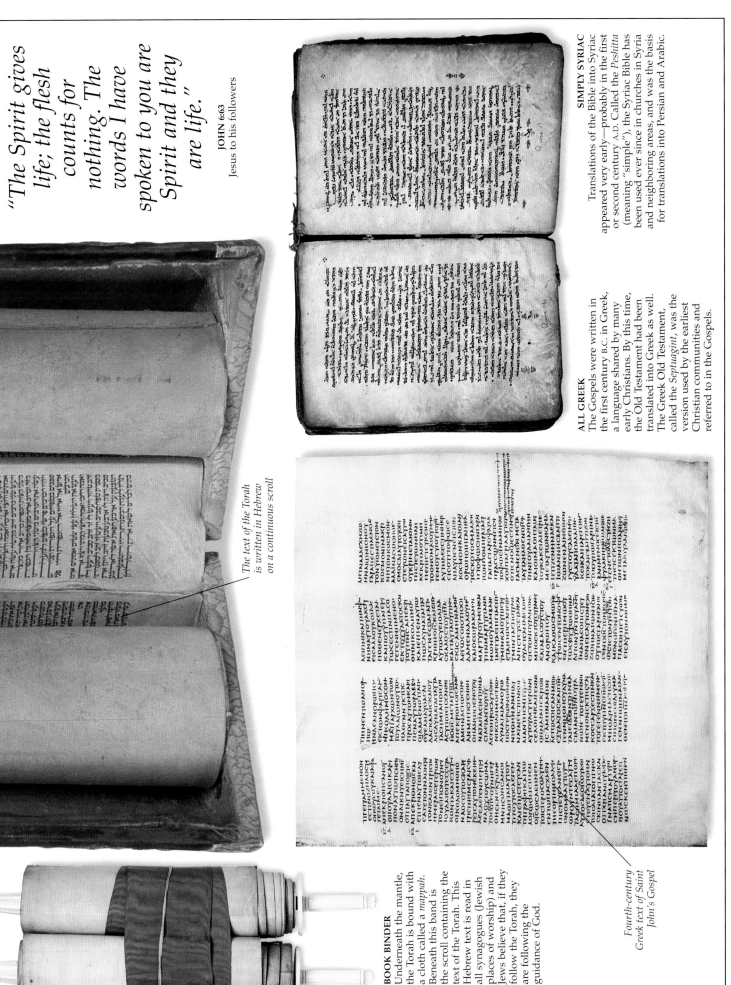

"The Spirit gives life; the flesh counts for nothing. The words I have spoken to you are Spirit and they are life."

JOHN 6:63
Jesus to his followers

The text of the Torah is written in Hebrew on a continuous scroll

SIMPLY SYRIAC
Translations of the Bible into Syriac appeared very early—probably in the first or second century A.D. Called the *Peshitta* (meaning "simple"), the Syriac Bible has been used ever since in churches in Syria and neighboring areas, and was the basis for translations into Persian and Arabic.

ALL GREEK
The Gospels were written in the first century B.C. in Greek, a language shared by many early Christians. By this time, the Old Testament had been translated into Greek as well. The Greek Old Testament, called the *Septuagint*, was the version used by the earliest Christian communities and referred to in the Gospels.

BOOK BINDER
Underneath the mantle, the Torah is bound with a cloth called a *mappah.* Beneath this band is the scroll containing the text of the Torah. This Hebrew text is read in all synagogues (Jewish places of worship) and Jews believe that, if they follow the Torah, they are following the guidance of God.

Fourth-century Greek text of Saint John's Gospel

Continued on next page

Heaven and Hell

ALL CHRISTIANS believe in one eternal and almighty God, who exists as three beings—the Father, the Son, and the Holy Spirit. They believe that Jesus is the Son of God, that he lived on Earth as the son of the Virgin Mary, and that he was crucified and rose from the dead. Christians have faith that if they follow the teachings of Jesus and repent their sins they will be rewarded after death with everlasting life in Heaven— the traditional name for God's eternal kingdom. Its opposite, the place or state without God, is known as Hell.

14th-century painting of the Holy Trinity by Andrei Roublev

THREE IN ONE
The idea of the Holy Trinity, the one God who exists as three beings, is one of the deepest mysteries of Christian faith. God the Father is the almighty creator of the universe. God the Son is Jesus, God made human. God the Holy Spirit is God's power on Earth. The Bible describes Jesus as sitting at God's right hand in Heaven.

This medieval illustration shows angels blowing their trumpets as the dead rise from their graves

LAST JUDGMENT
Christians look forward to a time when Jesus will return to Earth. They believe that he will come again in glory to judge the living and the dead. Jesus will reward the righteous with eternal life, and the kingdom of God will truly exist and have no end.

Angel carrying a golden censer

Ivory counter showing human figures fighting off the demons of Hell to ascend to Heaven, 1120

IN HEAVEN
For some, Heaven is a literal place, a paradise where God dwells. Others emphasize that Heaven is not a place, but a state of being with God forever. Catholics (pp. 28–31) believe that a person's soul goes first to a third place, called Purgatory, where it is purified before entering Heaven.

WINGED MESSENGERS
The Bible refers to angels as spiritual beings who live with God in Heaven. They act as messengers, bringing God's words and judgments to people on Earth and providing spiritual guidance. The Bible gives few clues about what angels look like, but they are traditionally portrayed as winged beings with human bodies.

JACOB'S LADDER

The life of Jacob, one of the ancestors of the people of Israel, is described in the Book of Genesis. Jacob had a dream in which he saw a ladder connecting Heaven and Earth. As Jacob watched angels passing up and down the ladder, God spoke and promised that the land where he slept would one day belong to him and his descendants.

Relief of Jacob's ladder, west front of Bath Abbey, England

Angel carrying a casket that may contain saintly relics (pp. 42–43)

Angel carrying a model church

Angels are often portrayed with shining, golden wings

THE FALL OF SATAN

According to the Book of Revelation, Satan— a member of the highest rank of angels, the archangels—started a war with God. As a result he was thrown out of Heaven and started his own evil kingdom in Hell. Some Christians believe Hell to be a place of pain, where Satan and his demons torture the souls of the damned, forcing them to endure everlasting fire.

DEVILISH DEPICTIONS

Since medieval times, artists have portrayed Satan and his demons as grotesque creatures, human in form but with horns, tails, and cloven hoofs. Most Christians today are less concerned with the appearance of Satan and Hell, and are more likely to think of the torture of Hell as the agony of an existence without the love of God.

Modern Mexican stamp depicting a devil

LOTERIA DE
MEXICO 1998 99
20¢

EL DIABLITO

G. NORMA / C. VERGARA   TIEV

The Reformation

DURING THE 14th and 15th centuries, many people in Europe were worried that the Catholic church was becoming corrupt. In the early 16th century three men—Martin Luther from Germany, Ulrich Zwingli from Switzerland, and John Calvin from France—spearheaded the reform of the church across Europe. In the movement now known as the Reformation, they and their followers founded new, Protestant churches. These churches rejected the control of the pope and bishops and stressed the importance of the Bible and preaching God's word.

Medal from the 1500s depicting the pope as Satan

CHURCH ABUSES
Reformers objected to several practices in the Catholic church. One of the most widespread abuses of the church was the use of indulgences—the payment of money instead of doing penance for sins. Even some popes were corrupt, and objectors often portrayed them as devil-like figures.

Bar, to screw down the platen

Platen, used to press the ink onto the paper

The coffin is pushed beneath the platen

Ink ball, to spread the ink evenly

AGAINST CORRUPTION
This coin was made in honor of Jan Hus, a Czech priest who became a reformer in the early 1400s. He spoke out against the corruption of the church but, despite support from ordinary people, was prevented from preaching, excommunicated, forced to leave Prague, and eventually burned at the stake.

EARLY IDEAS
Englishman John Wyclif, a theologian and politician, began to demand church reform in the late 14th century. Many of his ideas—such as the denial of the pope's authority and the call for the Bible to be translated into modern European languages—were taken up by later reformers all over Europe. In this painting by Ford Madox Brown, Wyclif is reading from his translation of the Bible.

PRINTING PRESS
In the 1450s, craftsman Johannes Gutenberg of Mainz, Germany, invented a new method of printing. It enabled books to be printed quickly and cheaply. This major advance allowed the ideas of the Reformation to travel around Europe at great speed.

VOICE OF REASON

Education developed rapidly at the time of the Reformation through the work of teachers like Desiderius Erasmus, shown here in a painting by Hans Holbein. His methods were different from Luther's passionate, revolutionary approach—he hoped to reform the church through reason and scholarship. Erasmus edited the Greek New Testament, which was a great help to the scholars who would later translate the Bible into modern European languages.

MOTHER TONGUE

In 1549, the Archbishop of Canterbury, Thomas Cranmer, published the *Book of Common Prayer*—a church service book in English. It enabled English people to hold services in their own language for the first time. When England briefly returned to Catholicism, under Queen Mary I in 1553, Cranmer was executed.

FAMOUS THESES

In October 1517, Martin Luther posted 95 theses (arguments against indulgences) on a church door in Wittenberg, Germany. He followed this with several books about reform. He argued that salvation came from God's grace through the individual's faith in Christ, and could not be bought.

Tympan, where the paper is put

Full- and pocket-sized copies of the *Book of Common Prayer*

CHURCH LEADER

In 1534, King Henry VIII forced the English church to break from Rome because the pope would not allow him to divorce his wife, Catherine of Aragon. Henry himself became leader of the English church, although, apart from his rejection of the pope, he remained Catholic in his beliefs. Despite this, he began the process that brought Protestantism to England.

Gallows, to support the tympan

Bolton Abbey, England

DISSOLUTION OF THE MONASTERIES

Henry VIII ordered his chief minister, Thomas Cromwell, to compile a report on the monasteries in England. Cromwell concluded that many were rich and corrupt, so Henry ordered all the monasteries to be dissolved (closed). He seized the wealth of the monasteries and gave many of their lands to his lords. Most of the monastery buildings, like Bolton Abbey, were left to become ruins.

16th-century portrait of Henry VIII by Hans Holbein the younger

Protestantism

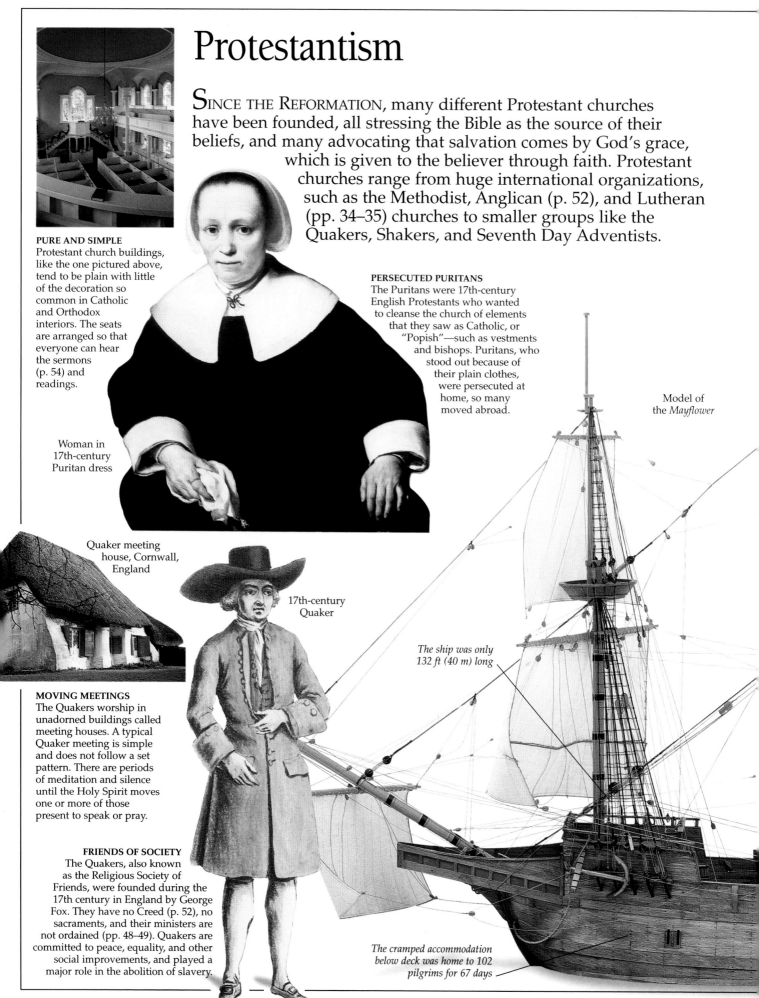

SINCE THE REFORMATION, many different Protestant churches have been founded, all stressing the Bible as the source of their beliefs, and many advocating that salvation comes by God's grace, which is given to the believer through faith. Protestant churches range from huge international organizations, such as the Methodist, Anglican (p. 52), and Lutheran (pp. 34–35) churches to smaller groups like the Quakers, Shakers, and Seventh Day Adventists.

PURE AND SIMPLE
Protestant church buildings, like the one pictured above, tend to be plain with little of the decoration so common in Catholic and Orthodox interiors. The seats are arranged so that everyone can hear the sermons (p. 54) and readings.

PERSECUTED PURITANS
The Puritans were 17th-century English Protestants who wanted to cleanse the church of elements that they saw as Catholic, or "Popish"—such as vestments and bishops. Puritans, who stood out because of their plain clothes, were persecuted at home, so many moved abroad.

Woman in 17th-century Puritan dress

Model of the *Mayflower*

Quaker meeting house, Cornwall, England

17th-century Quaker

The ship was only 132 ft (40 m) long

MOVING MEETINGS
The Quakers worship in unadorned buildings called meeting houses. A typical Quaker meeting is simple and does not follow a set pattern. There are periods of meditation and silence until the Holy Spirit moves one or more of those present to speak or pray.

FRIENDS OF SOCIETY
The Quakers, also known as the Religious Society of Friends, were founded during the 17th century in England by George Fox. They have no Creed (p. 52), no sacraments, and their ministers are not ordained (pp. 48–49). Quakers are committed to peace, equality, and other social improvements, and played a major role in the abolition of slavery.

The cramped accommodation below deck was home to 102 pilgrims for 67 days

A US Methodist Episcopal church

Wesley preaching the gospel, Wesley's Chapel, London, England

Cross of Saint George—the English flag

WORLDWIDE WORSHIP
The first Methodist churches were founded by the British preacher John Wesley in the mid-18th century. Since then, Methodism has spread all over the world. With independent branches like the Methodist Episcopal church in North America, Methodism has grown to become one of the largest Protestant groups.

TOURING PREACHER
Wesley was originally an Anglican clergyman who preached outside so that large numbers of people could hear him. He toured widely, preaching in both Britain and North America. This led to the founding of Methodist churches—groups of Christians who aimed to achieve holiness through the "method" laid down in the Bible.

Methodist Communion in Harare, Zimbabwe

JOYFUL WORSHIP
Worship in Methodist churches follows a pattern similar to that in Anglican and other Protestant churches, with hymns, prayers, Bible readings, a sermon, and the recital of the Creed. Within this framework, individuals in some churches stand up to affirm their faith with a joyful voice.

THE VOYAGE OF THE MAYFLOWER
In 1620, a group of Puritans from England and the Netherlands sailed to America on the *Mayflower*. After a hard voyage, the group, later known as the Pilgrims, landed in Massachusetts. Here they set up Plymouth Colony, a community where they could live and worship in their own way without fear of persecution.

Continued on next page

Shaker meeting with leader Mother Ann Lee, 1774

Salvation Army pin

THE SIMPLE LIFE
The Shaker movement reached its peak in the 19th century, and now there are very few Shakers. Members follow a simple lifestyle; they dress plainly, avoid alcohol and tobacco, and live in communities set apart from the outside world. Shakers are famous for the simple, well-made furniture that seems to sum up their way of life.

Shaker table and sewing chair

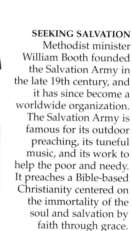

Member of the Salvation Army saluting God

SEEKING SALVATION
Methodist minister William Booth founded the Salvation Army in the late 19th century, and it has since become a worldwide organization. The Salvation Army is famous for its outdoor preaching, its tuneful music, and its work to help the poor and needy. It preaches a Bible-based Christianity centered on the immortality of the soul and salvation by faith through grace.

RESPECT YOUR ELDERS
There are a number of Presbyterian churches around the world, and they share one key feature—they are governed by presbyters, or elders, who may be either ministers or lay people. This kind of organization was based on the ideas of reformer John Calvin. Worship is simple and centers on preaching and— as shown in this 19th-century painting—study of the scriptures.

Salvation Army song
leader playing the cornet

*Salvation
Army tie*

Modern Salvation Army man's hat

SOLDIERS OF GOD
The Salvation Army is organized along
military lines. It is led by a "general," other
church leaders are known as "officers," and
members, or "soldiers," wear a distinctive
uniform. Those who enroll sign a declaration
of faith known as the "Articles of War."
All members are entitled to bear the
organization's red shield.

Victorian Salvation
Army woman's bonnet

THE HOLY LIFE
Founded by a follower
of the reformer Zwingli,
Mennonites aim to live a
life of holiness, set apart
from the world in self-
contained communities.
They are pacifists, and
they carry out relief
work in many parts
of the world.

*Red shield
badge*

Modern Salvation
Army woman's hat

Mennonite children in Belize

SEVENTH HEAVEN
Seventh Day Adventists, like
this couple in Mozambique,
believe that the time will come
when they will be taken to
Heaven for 1,000 years while
Satan rules on Earth. At the
end of this time, Jesus will
return, destroy Satan, and
create a new Earth. Adventists
operate schools and a network
of hospitals and clinics.

LIMITLESS WORSHIP
All Christians consider
the work of evangelism,
or spreading the Gospel,
to be part of their faith.
Many Protestants, like
these in Guatemala, are
very active evangelists.
They often worship and
preach outdoors, so their
congregations are not
limited by the size of a
church building, and
everyone who passes by
can hear their message.

The Christian life

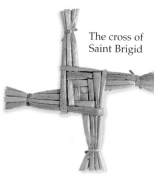

The cross of Saint Brigid

CHRISTIANS TRY TO FOLLOW Jesus' teachings and apply them to their own lives. All such believers are said to be part of the "community of saints." But some go to exceptional lengths for their faith, enduring suffering or persecution, or even becoming martyrs. Some of these men and women who have lived lives of special holiness are declared saints by the church. Saints are especially revered in the Catholic and Orthodox churches, where it is believed they can act as intermediaries between individual Christians and God.

FEEDING THE HUNGRY
Born in Ireland in the sixth century, Brigid became a nun and helped to spread Christianity by founding a monastery in Kildare. Brigid was famous for helping the poor, and was said to be able to make food multiply miraculously.

CHEATING DEATH
One of the many Christians who were persecuted by the Romans, Lucy remained true to her faith and gave away her possessions to the poor. The Romans were said to have tried to kill her by burning and by putting out her eyes. Lucy miraculously survived, and her eyes were restored. She was finally put to death by the sword.

Ivory relief of George and the dragon

Medieval gilded plaque of Saint Lucy

DRAGON SLAYER
George is thought to have been a third-century soldier from the eastern Mediterranean. The best-known story about him tells how a dragon was terrorizing the neighborhood and was about to devour the king's daughter. George said he would kill the monster if the people would believe in Jesus and be baptized. After killing the beast he would take no reward, but simply asked the king to help the church.

The palm is a symbol of the victory of the faithful over the enemies of the soul, and is often associated with martyrs

Eyes on a platter

40

SEEING THINGS
Hubert, the owner of this horn, lived in the eighth century and became a Christian after seeing a vision of the Crucifixion between the antlers of a stag while out hunting. From then on he devoted himself to converting others to Christianity in his native Belgium. He eventually became Bishop of Maastricht and Liège.

Plaster statue of Saint Joseph

A MAN OF INFLUENCE
Born in Algeria in 354, Augustine became one of the most influential theologians of all time. He was a lawyer and teacher before converting to Christianity in his thirties. His many books on subjects such as the Holy Trinity, charity, and the Psalms are still read today. He was also Bishop of Hippo in North Africa, as shown in this 15th-century painting.

16th-century painting of Saints Erasmus and Maurice

POPULAR SAINTS
Maurice, a soldier from Egypt, and Erasmus, a Syrian bishop, were martyred in the late third century. Although little is known of their lives, they were included in books of martyrs and became popular saints in the Middle Ages.

20TH-CENTURY SAINT
Italian Padre Pio was convinced of his "calling" as a child. When he became a Franciscan friar, he experienced visions of Jesus and received the stigmata—the miraculous appearance of wounds like those received by Jesus on the cross. Padre Pio endured his pain bravely, and devoted his life to prayer and serving God. He was declared a saint in 2002, 34 years after his death.

FAMILY LIFE
The family has a central role in Christian life. The Christian story begins with a family—Mary, Joseph, and Jesus—so it is seen by Christians as the ideal environment in which to raise children. This illustration shows a family walking to church on Christmas Eve.

JOSEPH THE PROTECTOR
As protector of the holy family, Joseph plays a vital part in the Christian story, and is especially revered in the Catholic church. Joseph is celebrated as the patron saint of fathers, carpenters, the dying, social justice, and the universal church.

HELPING HAND
Jesus told his followers to love their neighbors and give their wealth to the poor. Christians may follow these instructions through individual acts of kindness or through organizations that work to relieve suffering throughout the world.

Orphaned children helped by the Christian charity Tearfund

41

Continued on next page

Continued from previous page

Santiago de Compostela

The Virgin Mary
at Lourdes

Crown of semi-precious stones

PILGRIMAGE PLACES

Compostela in Spain and Lourdes in southwestern France are two of Europe's best-known pilgrimage sites. Compostela is said to be the burial place of Saint James, one of Jesus' disciples. Lourdes is a more recent shrine, the place where Saint Bernadette had a series of visions in the 19th century, and where many apparently miraculous healings have taken place.

Pilgrimages and relics

A pilgrimage is a journey to a place of religious significance. Many Christians, especially Roman Catholics, go on pilgrimages. They do so for various reasons—to visit places that are important for their faith, as an act of penance for their sins, to ask for help, or to give thanks to God. The most popular pilgrimage destinations are shrines. A shrine is a place linked to a particular saint, often housing their relics, or remains. Many sick people make pilgrimages to shrines such as Lourdes in the hope of a miraculous cure, but pilgrims are just as likely to travel in search of spiritual growth as physical healing.

The top lifted off to reveal the remains stored within

Wooden inner case—the true receptacle for the relics of Saint Eustace

Head is made of silver, but gilding gives it a golden color

Ornate outer case for the relics of Saint Eustace

The base of the casket is decorated with holy figures

INSIDE STORY

This elaborate reliquary was made in about 1240 to hold remains, which included some of the bones of Saint Eustace, an early Christian who converted to the faith after seeing a vision of the Crucifixion. The shining metal outer covering and wooden inner box did not contain Saint Eustace's whole skull, but held a number of bones, which were said to belong to several different saints.

CHAUCER'S PILGRIMS

In medieval England the shrine of Saint Thomas Becket at Canterbury was the most popular place of pilgrimage. The poet Geoffrey Chaucer wrote a long poem called *The Canterbury Tales*, made up of a series of stories told by a group of pilgrims as they traveled on horseback from London to Canterbury.

The Prioress

The Knight

The Man at Law

The Wife of Bath

The Squire

BECKET'S BONES

Thomas Becket was Archbishop of Canterbury in England during the reign of Henry II in the 12th century. When Becket fell out with the king, four of Henry's knights murdered him in Canterbury Cathedral. A shrine was soon built in the cathedral, and Becket's remains were kept in this beautiful casket.

Pewter badge of Saint Thomas Becket

Scallop-shaped ampulla, or flask, for holy water

One of the king's knights slices off Becket's head

Fragments of bone, wood, and fabric are beautifully displayed

MARK OF THE PILGRIM

In the Middle Ages, people often wore badges to show that they had been on a pilgrimage. The scallop shell, originally the badge of Compostela but later worn by pilgrims to any shrine, was the most common, but many places had their own badges.

INTO BATTLE

This reliquary, said to contain saintly bones, was carried into battle by the Abbot of Arbroath Abbey in Scotland. The occasion was the Battle of Bannockburn in 1314, when the Scottish, under their leader Robert Bruce, defeated the English.

Cross surrounded by pearls

Pieces of bone set in gold

TREASURED REMAINS

Relics do not have to be actual human remains. Fragments of objects that played a part in the Christian story are also revered. This collection of tiny relics, kept at a British Benedictine abbey, is said to include fragments of the cross, Jesus' crib, and the veil of the Virgin Mary, as well as relics of several saints.

PORTABLE RELICS

In the Middle Ages, some people carried holy relics around with them, in the hope that the remains would bring them closer to God. This small reliquary holds tiny pieces of the bones of saints, together with a small cross set among pearls. The use of gold and pearls in the reliquary reflects the high value of the items it contains.

Monks and nuns

NUN AND MONK
In the Middle Ages, new orders of monks and nuns were often founded because people felt the need to live by stricter rules than those governing other monasteries. Members of different orders, like this Servite nun and Slavonic monk, can often be distinguished by the color of their clothes.

FOR HUNDREDS OF YEARS, some Christians have felt the need to live separately from the rest of society, in special communities devoted to serving God. Such communities are called monasteries, and their inhabitants—monks or nuns—live a life that is harsher and stricter than normal. They make solemn vows to God of poverty, chastity, and obedience—promising to give up personal possessions and sexual relations and to obey both the head of the monastery (the abbot or abbess) and the set of rules by which they live. Monasticism plays an especially important part in the Catholic and Orthodox churches.

Modern-day Coptic monk

DESERT FATHERS
Monasticism began in Egypt in the third century, when men such as Saint Antony withdrew to the desert to live as hermits. These "desert fathers" eventually joined to form monasteries, and their traditions are carried on today by members of the Coptic church.

A SIMPLE LIFE
Saint Benedict wrote his rule at the monastery of Monte Cassino, Italy, in the 6th century. The rule imposes a simple life dominated by worship, prayer, reading, and work. It was adopted widely, and there are still a number of Benedictine monasteries today.

Church

Cloister gives access to main buildings and provides space for private study

Chapter house, where regular meetings are held

Refectory, where meals are taken

Herb and vegetable gardens

Gatehouse provides an entrance to the monastery

Dormitory, where the monks or nuns sleep

Outer wall cuts off building from the outside world

Infirmary, where the sick are treated

INSIDE A MONASTERY
A monastery has to provide somewhere for its monks or nuns to live, work, and worship. Traditionally, the main buildings are arranged around a courtyard called the cloister to one side of the church. These main buildings include a place to sleep, a place to eat, and a place in which to hold meetings. Fields and gardens for growing food are usually situated beyond the main complex.

THE WORK OF GOD
The most important activity for a monk or nun is regular religious observance at set hours of the day. Saint Benedict called this the "Work of God," but it is also known as the divine office. Everyone in the monastery meets eight times every day to pray, read lessons from the Bible, and sing hymns and Psalms.

15th-century monastic service book

FIGHTING MONKS
In the Middle Ages there were specialized orders of "fighting monks," who lived by monastic rules and gave armed protection to pilgrims in the Holy Land. This gunpowder flask bears the emblem of one such order, the Knights of Saint John.

Benedictine monk in quiet contemplation

Poor Clares—
Franciscan nuns

PRIVATE PRAYER
Individual worship plays a vital part in the daily life of all monks and nuns. These Franciscan nuns—known as Poor Clares after their founder, Saint Clare—are praying the rosary. Some orders count their prayers using knots on a piece of rope instead of rosary beads.

DIVINE LIGHT
Several of the "hours" of the divine office are celebrated when it is dark. Matins takes place at 2 AM, vespers during the evening, and compline before bedtime. Traditionally, worship at such times had to be celebrated by candlelight. The candles would also have reminded those taking part of the idea of Jesus as a divine light shining in the world.

HOLY READING
Benedictine monks are encouraged to read the Bible (and other religious writings) in a devotional, contemplative way to bring them into close communion with God. This activity, known as *Lectio Divina* (holy reading), does not involve analyzing the text, as some Bible-reading does. The reader should simply absorb the words and allow God's message to filter through.

Continued on next page

Continued from previous page

Lemon balm

Marjoram Lungwort

Feverfew

HEALING HERBS
In the Middle Ages, monks grew plants like feverfew, lungwort, lemon balm, and marjoram to make medicines for ailments such as headaches and respiratory disorders. The monks wrote down their discoveries about the healing powers of plants in books called herbals. Herbs are still grown alongside other food plants in many monastery gardens today.

Everyday life and work
Although the divine office and prayer are at the heart of monastic life, monks and nuns are also expected to work hard to support themselves and their community. Monasteries often try to be as self-sufficient as possible, with many producing their own food, and some making items for sale. With their atmosphere of quiet contemplation, monasteries have always been centers of learning. In the Middle Ages, they provided Europe's only education and health services, and today many monks and nuns still teach in schools. They may also work in the wider community, giving aid to the sick, poor, and needy.

Benedictine monks in the refectory

FOOD FOR THOUGHT
In most monasteries, the monks or nuns eat together at long tables in a large communal refectory, or dining room. The food is simple but nourishing. Religious devotion even continues at meal times—everyone is expected to eat in silence while one of their number reads passages from the Bible.

SCENTED SERVICES
Incense—a substance that makes a sweet scent when it is burned—is used widely during services in both the Catholic and Orthodox churches. Some monasteries make incense, both for use in their own church and for sale to raise money.

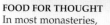

Raw olibanum gum

Ground raw olibanum gum

Finished incense

1 NATURALLY SWEET
The naturally sweet-smelling raw olibanum gum is ground into smaller pieces. The monk then measures out a small amount of concentrated perfume oil and mixes this thoroughly with the ground gum.

Rubber gloves provide protection from the highly concentrated oil

2 DRYING OUT
The monk places shovels of the scented, ground gum into a large, wooden tray with a wire bottom and spreads it out evenly. He leaves the incense mixture until it is dry and then packs it up ready for sale.

Wafer press and wafers decorated with Christian symbols

FLAT BREAD
In many churches, specially made wafers—traditionally manufactured in monasteries—are used instead of ordinary bread during Communion (pp. 52–53). The process starts with a bread dough mix. This is pressed into thin sheets, often marked with a Christian symbol, and cut into small disks. The finished wafers are then packaged and supplied to churches all over the world.

FAR FROM HOME
Many monks and nuns travel long distances to take part in aid programs in areas that are affected by drought, war, famine, or other disasters. Members of monastic orders help to save lives and bring education to areas where there are no public schools.

Nun distributing cooking oil in Rwanda

The text is in Latin and is beautifully decorated

The desk slopes to make writing for long periods more comfortable

The nun studies the honeycomb to see if it is ready for harvesting

Monastic scribe's desk

WRITING FOR GOD
In the Middle Ages, monks and nuns were among the few people who produced books. They wrote out each page by hand and decorated them to produce results like this beautiful music manuscript. Today, some monks preserve these ancient skills, while others are notable scholars. They write books on subjects such as the Bible, theology, and the history of the church.

Wax tablet for writing holy passages on

The angel's banner says "With the Lord a thousand years is a single day"

SWEET AND SYMBOLIC
Honey is an ancient Christian symbol that reminds the faithful of the sweetness of Jesus' words. This Franciscan nun has learned the valuable skill of beekeeping, providing a nutritious food source for her sisters and beeswax for making candles. Many monks and nuns sell any honey and wax they do not use themselves to members of the public.

Plate made to commemorate the year 2000

CHRISTIAN EARTHENWARE
The pottery founded by the Benedictine monks of Prinknash Abbey in England produces simple wares for everyday use, and more decorative ceramics that are especially attractive to visitors. Their millennium plate bears a picture of an angel, a reminder that the year 2000 was, above all, a Christian event— the 2,000th anniversary of Jesus' birth.

"...in everything, by prayer and petition, with thanksgiving, present your requests to God."

PHILIPPIANS 4:6
Paul in his letter to the church at Philippi

Christian culture

ARTISTS, WRITERS, AND MUSICIANS have been responding to the Christian message for 2,000 years. Very early in the history of Christianity, people were decorating church walls and writing music for use during services. Soon, much of the art produced in the Western world was Christian, and as the faith spread around the world, its influence on art followed. There are fewer Christian artists today, but Christianity still influences both our art and lives.

We swear oaths in court, listen to gospel music, watch movies based on Bible stories, and see paintings, statues, and buildings that rework Christian subjects in exciting new ways.

SOLEMN PROMISES
In Christian cultures, the most solemn, binding promise is an oath sworn on the Bible, "by almighty God." A court official like this judge swears to do his job to the best of his ability. A witness in court swears to tell the entire truth.

The visual arts

From paintings and statues of Jesus to soaring cathedrals that seem to reach to the heavens, Christianity has had a huge impact on the visual arts. Most famous examples date from earlier times, but visual artists are still being inspired by the faith. Some make art to adorn churches, and others draw on Christian imagery to produce works for a wider public.

CHRIST OF RIO
Completed in 1931, *Christ the Redeemer* stands more than 100 ft (30 m) tall and overlooks Rio de Janeiro, Brazil. It was designed by artist Carlos Oswaldo and carved from soapstone, which, although quite soft, is resistant to weather damage. From the top of the rocky outcrop of Corcovado, the statue dominates the city and has become known the world over as a symbol of Rio.

The wings are tilted forward to give a sense of embrace

STEEL ANGEL
Antony Gormley's *Angel of the North*, which stands in Gateshead in England, has wings 175 ft (54 m) wide—similar in size to the wings of a jumbo jet. This modern angel, completed in 1998, is seen by thousands of travelers on the road and railroad line that pass the site. Made of a special steel that contains copper, the statue has a rich reddish-brown color that stands out against the sky.

GLASSY GLORY
Popular since the early Middle Ages, stained glass windows flood the interiors of many churches with beautiful colored light. This spectacular spiral window, leading the eye up toward the heavens, is a modern take on this old tradition. Installed in 1996 at Thanksgiving Chapel in Dallas, Texas, the *Glory Window* was designed by French artist Gabriel Loire.

UNDER CONSTRUCTION
Most of the world's cathedrals were finished long ago, but a few are still being built. Barcelona's vast cathedral of the Sagrada Familia (Holy Family) was designed by Catalan architect Antoni Gaudí. Construction began in the 1880s, but the huge building project continues to this day.

THE NINE SAINTS
Modern New York painter and illustrator Laura James is inspired by the art of Ethiopia, and in her painting of nine Ethiopian saints she hopes to introduce people to the history of this country. Christianity came to Ethiopia in the fourth century, so the artist has a long tradition from which to draw inspiration.

Continued on next page

ACTING WITH PASSION

In some parts of Europe, local people put on traditional plays enacting the story of the Passion—the events leading up to Jesus' crucifixion. In the village of Oberammergau in southern Germany, the Passion play has been staged regularly ever since the people escaped the plague in 1633. The play is now produced every ten years.

This scene is set in the disciple Simon's house

The performing arts

Music has been a part of Christian worship for centuries, and many composers in the Middle Ages were monks who spent their lives writing and singing church music. But from the beginning, religious music influenced other types of music, from extravagant choral pieces to dances and popular songs. Drama has also been influenced by Christianity for hundreds of years, and there are many famous movies and plays with religious themes.

The parting of the Red Sea

Moses

Rameses II

FROM STAGE TO SCREEN

The "rock opera" *Jesus Christ Superstar* was first staged in 1970, and made into a movie in 1973. With music by Andrew Lloyd Webber and words by Tim Rice, the production was one of the most popular 20th-century treatments of the Christian story.

EPIC MOVIE

The Ten Commandments—a movie created in 1956 by Hollywood director Cecil B. de Mille—tells how Moses led his people out of slavery in Egypt to their promised homeland. It features a huge cast, with Charlton Heston as Moses and Yul Brynner as Rameses II, and spectacular special effects, such as the parting of the Red Sea to let the Israelites pass.

"Shout for joy to the Lord, all the earth. Worship the Lord with gladness; come before him with joyful songs."

PSALM 100:1–2
A hymn of praise

Sacred oratorios (a blend of solo and choral music) became popular in the 18th century. Among the most famous are J. S. Bach's two settings of the Passion story and G. F. Handel's *Messiah*. Handel wrote the piece in less than four weeks in 1741, and its portrayal of Jesus' life is still enjoyed by audiences today, especially around Christmas time.

Handel's original score of *Messiah*

GRACEFUL GOSPEL
Soul singer Aretha Franklin is the daughter of a preacher and a gospel singer from Detroit. She sang with her father's choir before starting to make her own records. Her music is powerfully emotional and full of strong vocal effects, showing her roots in gospel music. Her album *Amazing Grace* is a collection of reworked gospel songs.

Gospel choir performing in Washington, D.C.

MUSICAL CONVERSATION
Baptist churches in the US are the original home of gospel music, in which the preacher and congregation create an emotional musical conversation. The excitement of gospel music, with its sliding melodies, joyful shouts, and other vocal effects, has had a huge influence on singers in many diverse areas of modern music, from soul to rock.

THE KING
Rock and roll legend Elvis Presley learned to sing in his local church choir, and was influenced by gospel music. He combined this with rhythm and blues and country music to create a unique style. Later in his career, he recorded unique versions of a number of hymns and carols.

Did you know?

AMAZING FACTS

As head of the Roman Catholic Church, popes can lead luxurious lifestyles. Unlike his predecessor John Paul II, whose modest wardrobe included Dr. Marten's shoes, Pope Benedict XVI has been spotted in designer sunglasses and red Prada shoes.

Benedict XVI

Many popular children's books are based on the Christian experience, including C. S. Lewis's Chronicles of Narnia series. In Narnia, Aslan the lion symbolizes Christ, and the adventures of Aslan and the other characters mirror the struggles of Christians to destroy evil and reach the kingdom of heaven.

Vatican City is more than a city; with complete political autonomy, it is the smallest independent state in the world.

Many of the world's most important civil rights leaders have begun as Christian ministers, including Reverend Martin Luther King Jr., who led the civil rights movement in the United States, and Archbishop Desmond Tutu, who won the Nobel Peace Prize in 1984 for his work against apartheid in South Africa.

Archbishop Desmond Tutu

The father of evolution, Charles Darwin, was training to be a priest before his scientific pursuits led him to write *The Origin of Species*. He initially delayed releasing his theory to avoid controversy, but eventually published it in the hope that people would accept religion and science as part of the same worldview. Darwin remained a devout Christian throughout his life, but his theories are the subject of debate to this day.

IΧΘΥC

The fish symbol and "ichthys" label

Early Christians used secret symbols to help them communicate and worship without persecution. One way of encoding Jesus's name was a fish symbol—the Greek word for fish, *ichthys*, can also stand for "Jesus Christ, Son of God, Savior." In the year 312, Christians were given official permission to worship in public, but many of these coded signs are still used in church iconography.

Martin Luther, renowned for igniting the Protestant movement, also contributed to the popularization of the church by translating the Bible into his native German (at a rate of more than 1,500 words per day!) and authoring some of Christianity's most beloved hymns.

About 75% of Americans identify themselves as Christians. In the United States and Canada, Christians outnumber Jews and Muslims by about 40 to 1.

Since the fourth century, bishops have worn purple as a symbol of their status. Purple, made from an expensive dye, was once worn only by the Roman emperor and his senators. The bishops' purple sash showed that they had all the rights and privileges that Roman senators did.

In the fifth century, the monk Dionysius the Short introduced a new Christian calendar centered around Jesus's birth, with the terms AD, or year of our Lord, and BC, or before Christ. We still use that system today (sometimes using the terms BCE, or Before the Common Era, and CE, or Common Era)—but we now know that Dionysius had Jesus's birthday wrong by at least three years.

As the number of Christians declines in Europe and America and rises in Africa, Latin America, and Asia, the center of the Christian world is shifting to the "Global South." By the year 2025, it's predicted that about 80 percent of the world's Roman Catholics will be Latin American or African.

Christian rock is one of the fastest-growing genres in terms of music sales since the year 2000. Some very famous faces have gotten their start as Christian singers, including Jessica Simpson and Amy Grant.

The Catholic church divides holy relics into three categories: A first-class relic is either part of a saint's body or an object directly relating to the events of a saint's life. A second-class relic is an object or article of clothing owned by a saint. A third-class relic is a piece of cloth touched to the body of a saint after death, or else brought to a saint's shrine.

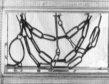

St. Peter's chains, a first-class relic

An important duty of early monks was the copying of the scriptures by hand onto illuminated, or illustrated, pages. The detailed artwork used pigments made from precious metals and stones, such as gold and lapis lazuli—a stone so rare that its rich blue was reserved for coloring the robes of the Virgin Mary.

Mary in blue robes

Q What is the "Christian Right?"

A The Christian Right is an American branch of Christianity with conservative social and political views. Its members are known for their opposition to social and legal policies that they see as un-Christian, such as abortion and evolutionary teachings in schools. They are unique among American Christians in that they have the goal—and in some cases the power—of bringing religion into government in order to protect and promote conservative values.

Jerry Falwell of the Christian Right

Q How is the pope chosen?

A After the death of a pope, a conclave of cardinals gathers at the Vatican to elect a new pope. The cardinals cast votes on paper ballots, which are counted and then burned. If no candidate has received two-thirds of the vote, straw is mixed into the fire so that the smoke from the chimney burns black to signal that the election was not conclusive. When a new pope is finally elected, the smoke from the chimney burns white.

Smoke signaling the election of a pope

Q What are the sacraments?

A The sacraments—baptism, Eucharist, confirmation, marriage, and holy orders—are Christian rites of passage. (Catholics also include confession and anointing of the sick.) Most Protestants believe that sacraments represent the sacred. Anglicans and Catholics hold that the sacraments bestow grace directly.

Q How long did it take to build a Gothic cathedral?

A The Gothic cathedrals that came into fashion in the 12th century were so massive and ornate that funds often ran out before they could be finished. For this reason as well as the sheer amount of labor required, one church could take centuries to build. Cologne Cathedral in Germany took more than 700 years to complete.

Q What religions are part of Christianity?

A The major Christian denominations include Roman Catholics, Orthodox Christians, Baptists, Anglicans (or Episcopalians), Lutherans, Presbyterians, and Methodists. There are also smaller groups within Christianity, but most share the unifying principle of belief in the trinity of Father, Son, and Holy Spirit.

Q Why do the colors on the altar and on a priest's vestments change from week to week?

A Every church season has its own color, which is chosen to suit the mood of a time. For instance, during Lent, colors are very subdued and dark as Christians are asked to make sacrifices and prepare for Easter. On Easter Sunday, the colors change to a vibrant white to reflect the joyfulness of that day and season.

Q How many popes have there been?

A There have been 265 popes of the Roman Catholic church (263, if you don't count the second and third times Benedict IX was elected). That includes 205 Italians, 19 Frenchmen, 14 Greeks, 8 Syrians, 6 Germans, 3 Africans, 2 Spaniards, an Austrian, a Palestinian, an Englishman, a Dutchman, and a Pole.

Q How was the New Testament compiled?

A In 367 AD, the Epistle of Athanasius proposed a list of books to be included in the New Testament. There were 27 books chosen—but many others, both in writing and in oral tradition, were left out. These banned books, which include a different version of the Garden of Eden story, are known as the Apocrypha.

Flying buttresses support much of the weight of the ornate construction.

Cologne Cathedral

Q Can any bread become communion?

A A priest's blessing makes any bread suitable for communion. However, most churches choose to use very simple, unleavened bread, which is what Jesus would have blessed at the Last Supper.

Communion wafers

Record Breakers

LARGEST CATHEDRAL
The Cathedral of St. John the Divine in New York City measures 121,000 square feet (36,880 square meters)—the size of two football fields.

LONGEST-REIGNING POPE
Some consider St. Peter to be the longest-reigning pope, since he served for up to 34 years. Others give the title to Pius IX, who served for 31 years starting in 1846.

OLDEST CHURCH
Remains of the oldest known church built specifically as a Christian place of worship were found in Aqaba, Jordan, and date from the late third century.

MOST POPULAR HYMN
According to an online poll, the most popular hymn is *Amazing Grace*, composed in the 18th century by John Newton.

LARGEST BIBLE
The world's largest Bible is 43 ½ in (1.1 m) tall, with a spine 34 in (86 cm) thick. It weighs in at 1,094 pounds (496 kg).

Timeline

THE REAL STORY OF CHRISTIANITY STARTS at the beginning of time, with the first evidence of God's hand on Earth. The pivotal event, however, is the birth of Christ. Documents from those early years disagree about some of the dates, so it can be hard to pin down exact years with certainty, but the overall chronology is a fascinating journey of mystery and miracles, and a remarkable insight into the history of the Western world.

Constantine

c. 2100 BC

The story of "modern" man begins in the Book of Genesis, when God visits Abraham and promises him that he will be the father of nations, and that Canaan will be his home.

c. 1250 BC

Moses leads the Exodus from Egypt and receives the Ten Commandments.

Moses holding the Ten Commandments

37 BC

Herod is appointed sole ruler of Judea as a friend of the Roman Empire. Although he is technically the king of the Jews, he is not of Jewish ancestry, and many of his orthodox subjects are unhappy with his reign. Still, he wins some local support though his building projects, including a grand temple.

31 BC

Octavian, Julius Caesar's adopted son, takes control of Rome. He will become known as Augustus, the emperor who required the census that forced Joseph and Mary to travel to Bethlehem. Augustus will rule the Roman Empire until his death in 14 AD.

c. 4 BC

Jesus is born.

The Holy Family

4 BC

After his reign descends into terror in its later years, Herod dies. His kingdom is divided among his sons.

c. 26 AD

At age 27, John the Baptist, Jesus's cousin, begins his ministry. He famously wears a coarse camel-hair shirt and lives on locusts and honey. Most importantly, he performs baptisms and entreats the people of Jerusalem to prepare for the coming of Jesus. He later baptizes Jesus himself.

c. 27 AD

Jesus is baptized and begins his ministry. He chooses his disciples and performs his first miracle at the wedding at Canaan.

c. 30 AD

Jesus is crucified.

c. 49 AD

The Council of Jerusalem, presided over by Peter and attended by all the apostles, decides that many Jewish laws, such as the requirement of circumcision and dietary restrictions, do not apply to Christian converts.

70 AD

A Jewish rebellion against Roman rule ends with the Fall of Jerusalem. About 600,000 people are killed, and much of the city is destroyed, including Herod's temple.

c. 120 AD

The Didache, a kind of handbook for Christians, is written, and probably used in missionary work.

202–311 AD

During these tumultuous years, Christians are often out of favor with the Roman Empire, which has become less tolerant of religious diversity.

312 AD

Emperor Constantine converts to Christianity. He later decrees in the Edict of Milan (313 AD) that all Roman subjects are free to worship as they please.

325 AD

The Council of Nicaea, attended by about 300 bishops, creates the Nicene Creed, which lays out Christian beliefs about the nature of the Father, Son, and Holy Spirit.

367 AD

Athanasius lists the 27 books that will be included in the New Testament.

380 AD

Christianity is made the official religion of the Roman Empire.

382–405 AD

Jerome works on the Vulgate, a translation of the complete Bible from its Hebrew, Aramaic, and Greek parts into a single Latin volume. The work, commissioned by Pope Damascus, took its name from the Latin word *vulgus*, or "common people."

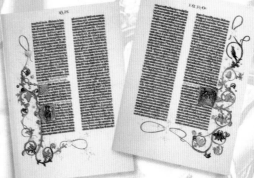

Pages from a 15th-century Vulgate

787 AD

The Second Council of Nicaea lays out codes of behavior for monks and members of the clergy, requiring that bishops thoroughly read the scriptures and forbidding monks from building houses of worship without first procuring funds.

Anti-evolution Christians selling books st the opening of the Scopes trial

1054

As the Western church concentrates its power in Rome, the church in the East is increasingly alienated and often disagrees with Rome's decisions on such matters as the ecclesiastical calendar and amendments to the Nicene Creed. The disagreements finally come to a head when Pope Leo IX and Patriarch Michael Cerularius excommunicate each other in the event that has become known as the Great Schism.

1095

At the Council of Clermont, Pope Urban II claims that the Turks have invaded Christian lands and committed unspeakable horrors against innocent Christians. In fact, the Turks are reported to have treated Christians fairly, but Urban's speech, designed to benefit his Arab allies, succeeds in inciting Christians to drive back the Turks and recover the Holy Land in the First Crusade. Seven Crusades will eventually rage through Europe, lasting until the late 13th century and costing thousands of lives.

1215

The Fourth Lateran Council defines the transubstantiation of the Eucharist, and requires all Catholics to receive communion on Easter or face excommunication.

1378–1423

A hasty and somewhat inconclusive conclave elects Urban VI. The fallout of this too-informal election leads to a new conclave, a new election, and a second pope, who will be installed in Avignon, France. The Western Schism brought about by these events is finally resolved almost 50 years later when the papacy is firmly re-established in Rome.

1431

After responding to divine inspiration and leading the armies of France, Joan of Arc becomes a martyr when she is burned at the stake for witchcraft.

Joan of Arc

1517

Martin Luther nails his 95 Theses to the door of Wittenberg Church in Germany, criticizing what he sees as the corrupt and elitist practices of the church, and giving rise to the Protestant Reformation.

1534

Henry VIII's Act of Supremacy establishes the English monarch as head of the church in Great Britain, supplanting the power of the pope in England.

1536

John Calvin publishes his protestant ideas as *Institutes of the Christian Religion*, drawing anti-Protestant criticism and forcing him to flee to Geneva. His most influential belief is the idea of predestination, by which a person is admitted to or rejected from heaven based purely on whether or not he or she was born with grace, regardless of good works.

1734

Under the leadership of Massachusetts preacher Jonathan Edwards, the Great Awakening marks a new wave of piety in the United States, in response to the scientific advances of the Enlightenment.

1841

David Livingstone, a Scottish explorer-missionary, travels to Africa for the first time. Over the course of his life, he will be responsible for setting up numerous Christian missions on the continent.

1854

The Dogma of Immaculate Conception asserts that Mary was born free from the taint of original sin. This issue had been debated within the church for centuries.

1869

The First Vatican Council is attended by about 800 church leaders from around the world. Its most important result is the Dogma of Papal Infallibility, which states that certain decrees of the pope are correct by definition.

1925

In the "Scopes Monkey Trial," the opposition of certain Christian fundamentalists to Darwin's theory of evolution gains national attention in the United States for the first time.

1948

The World Council of Churches holds its first meeting. The council is part of the ecumenical movement, which strives to promote unity between different factions of Christianity.

1962–65

The Second Vatican Council introduces reforms in Catholic practice, including a more accessible mass and less formal habits for nuns.

1978

Pope John Paul II begins his reign, soon becoming one of the most beloved and popular pontiffs in recent history.

Bishop Harris

1989

Barbara Clementine Harris of Massachusetts is ordained as the first female bishop in an Anglican church.

2005

Benedict XVI is elected pope.

Find out more

WHETHER YOUR COMMUNITY HAS ACCESS to world-class museums or a single church, there are plenty of opportunities to learn more about Christianity. Often the best place to start is at a church near you, which may have youth programs, educational series, or musical performances year round. Museums are a wonderful opportunity to see ancient religious art up close, and get a feel for what things were really like in the early days of the church. And of course the Web is full of resources that are just a click away. Check out the information on these pages for ideas about how to learn more.

GO TO MUSEUMS
Most major museums have exhibits of religious art and artifacts. Look for paintings of Mary and Jesus, stained glass, chalices, and even full altars in some museums. You'll learn to recognize some themes that recur again and again.

A young member of the church playing an angel in the Nativity

PARTICIPATE IN YOUTH GROUPS
Local churches can help you find Christian youth groups in your area—or try the phone book or Internet to find an organization nearby. Many youth groups spend time reading the scriptures together or discussing the readings and sermons from the week's church service. Some also put on special holiday programs and are active volunteers in their communities.

LOOK TO THE BIBLE
There are lots of different versions of the Bible, so if you find yours difficult to understand, visit a Christian bookstore for help finding one that's more accessible. Some even come with illustrations or study guides to help you get the most out of the scriptures.

USEFUL WEB SITES

www.christianitytoday.com
Chock full of articles and information about contemporary Christian issues
www.vatican.va
Includes information about the Pope, biographies of the saints, daily news updates from Rome, a map of Vatican City, and more
www.adherents.com
Features U.S. census and survey information about religious topics
www.religionfacts.com
A comparison chart, holiday descriptions, key to symbols, and lots of history and cool facts about Christianity

VISIT A CHURCH

Visit churches in your community to see different styles of worship and church architecture (such as that of the Cathedral of Our Lady of the Angels in Los Angeles, right). Regular services are open to everyone, so you can observe the practices of another denomination. Just be sensitive—you may want to stay in your seat during communion or other blessings.

ENJOY CHURCH MUSIC

If your church has a resident choir, find out when their performances will be and listen in. Or you can seek out another choir by checking a local events calendar. Most church music was written for a specific purpose—such as a funeral or wedding—so it can be interesting to do some research about the piece you're about to hear to help you put it in context.

WATCH MOVIES

Throughout the years, movies have always returned to the religious themes that intrigue audiences. Musicals such as *Godspell* are old favorites that treat Jesus's story with a lighter touch. In 2004, *The Passion of the Christ* created controversy with the graphic violence and suffering in its more literal portrayal of the Crucifixion.

Places to visit

NATIONAL CATHEDRAL, WASHINGTON, D.C.
Conceived during George Washington's presidency, this impressive cathedral was built as a house of prayer for all Americans and a site for events of national importance, such as presidential funerals and speeches from inspirational leaders. Construction spanned 83 years and was completed in 1990.

THE CLOISTERS, NEW YORK, NY
This monastery has been reconstructed from medieval architectural elements. Most of the building itself as well as its impressive collection of religious art was transported from European sites. The museum includes a chapel, courtyard, and garden that let visitors see what monastic life really looked like in the Middle Ages.

ST. LOUIS CATHEDRAL, NEW ORLEANS, LA
The oldest cathedral in the United States, St. Louis Cathedral was established in 1720. A recent renovation has restored the beautiful frescoes and artwork that make a visit to this church special. Also nearby is Ursuline Convent, the oldest French colonial building in the United States and home to the pioneering Ursuline nuns.

THE ALAMO, SAN ANTONIO, TX
The site made famous by its role in the Texas Revolution was originally built in 1744 as a mission for the education of American Indians who had converted to Christianity. Take a tour through its serene grounds to see how the Texan missionaries lived, then walk to four other nearby missions that are part of the San Antonio Missions National Historic Park.

PENNSYLVANIA DUTCH COUNTRY, LANCASTER COUNTY, PA
Lancaster County is home to communities of Amish Christians that have remained largely unchanged since their arrival in the early 1700s. Visitors can visit an Amish home, a farm, and a one-room schoolhouse, and even take an Amish buggy ride to learn more about their faith and slower-paced way of life.

Glossary

ABBOT/ABBESS The head of a community of monks or nuns

ALTAR a raised table- or tomblike structure at the east end of a church where bread and wine are consecrated

ANGEL A spiritual being who may act as a guardian to humans or as a messenger from God

Angel

ANNUNCIATION An announcement, specifically the announcement that Mary would bear the son of God

ANOINTING The act of conferring a blessing, typically by making the sign of the cross on a person's skin with oil or water

APOSTLE A missionary, a supporter, or a person sent to spread the word of Christ; specifically, one of Jesus's 12 companions during his lifetime

ASPERGILLUM A small, perforated ball or brush used for sprinkling holy water during church services

ASSUMPTION The taking of a soul into heaven. The religious holiday called the Feast of the Assumption celebrates the taking of Mary's soul into Heaven.

BAPTISM A sacrament in which holy water is used to bless a new member of the church and "wash away" his or her original sin

BISHOP A clergyperson ranking above a priest, often the governor of a diocese and supervisor of other local religious personnel

CARDINAL The highest level of Roman Catholic clergy under the pope. Cardinals may have appointed roles at the Vatican, and also have duties to their home parishes.

CATACOMBS Underground cemeteries made up of cavelike hallways and recessed tombs. In the years when the practice of Christianity was illegal, many Christians used the obscurity of catacombs to worship in secret.

CATHEDRAL A usually large, opulent church that is the official seat of a diocese. The name is derived from *cathedra*, which is the Latin word for "throne," or the official seat of a bishop.

CHALICE A ceremonial cup from which communion wine is taken

CONFESSION A sacrament in which a person confesses his or her sins in order to be absolved, or forgiven. In the Catholic tradition, a priest hears confession before granting absolution. In the Protestant tradition, the sincere act of confession itself is believed to achieve absolution.

COWL The hood or long-hooded cloak worn by a monk

CROZIER A symbol of a bishop's or abbot's office; a tall staff shaped like a shepherd's crook

CRUCIFIXION The act of executing a person by hanging them on a cross; specifically, Jesus's death on the cross

DENOMINATION An organized group of Christians that adheres to a certain set of practices and beliefs

DOGMA A decree handed down as an absolute truth from the pope

ENCYCLICAL An official letter from the pope

EPISTLE A letter, especially a formal or official letter

Catacomb

EUCHARIST Another word for communion; the re-enactment of Christ's sharing of bread and wine as his body and blood at the Last Supper

EXCOMMUNICATE To expel from membership in the church

GOOD SAMARITAN Like the character in the parable, someone who is ready and willing to help another person, even if the person is a stranger or an enemy

GOSPEL One of the first four books of the New Testament, which present the story of Jesus Christ, and discuss the kingdom of God and salvation; a reading from one of the four Gospel books. A gospel reading is included as a reading in most church services.

GRACE A spiritual state of being closer to God; divine assistance or virtue given by God; a prayer said before meals

HABIT A nun's uniform

HERETIC A baptized person who speaks or acts against God or church doctrine

HOLY ORDERS The sacrament of becoming a priest, nun, or other minister of the church

HOLY WATER Water that has been blessed by a priest to be used in church services

ILLUMINATED MANUSCRIPT A handwritten book whose pages are illustrated with colorful, intricate artwork, usually by scribes in a monastery

INDULGENCE A "credit" for grace or absolution that was once sold to parishioners by Catholic church officials

Chalice

MAGI The three Eastern kings, or wise men, who visited the baby Jesus in Bethlehem

Magi

MANGER A trough from which animals eat

MANTLE A loose, sleeveless overgarment worn by priests during church services

MARTYR A person who voluntarily suffers death rather than renounce his or her religious beliefs; to kill a person who refuses to renounce his or her beliefs

MESSIAH The awaited savior of the Jews; a name for Christ

MIRACLE An occurrence that cannot be explained by the laws of nature, and is attributed to the will of God or a saint

MITER A tall, pointed headdress worn by bishops and abbots

MONASTERY A place where monks live as a community

MONK A man who is a member of a religious community and has taken a vow of poverty, chastity, and obedience

MYRRH A kind of fragrant resin; one of the gifts brought to the baby Jesus by the magi

NUN A woman who is a member of a religious community and has taken a vow of poverty, chastity, and obedience

ORTHODOX Conservative; specifically, some Eastern branches of Christianity

PAGAN A person who does not acknowledge the God of the Bible; usually has negative connotations

PARABLE A story told to teach a lesson

PATEN A ceremonial plate used to carry bread for the Eucharist

PIETÁ A scene, often depicted in religious artwork, of Mary holding the dead Jesus after he has been taken down from the cross

PILGRIM A person who travels to a place or along a route for the purpose of worship

POPE The elected head of the Catholic church

PRIEST A person ordained to lead church services and perform sacraments

PSALM A sacred song or poem

PSALTER A book of psalms for devotional use

PULPIT A podium in a church from which readings or sermons are delivered

PURGATORY According to Catholic belief, a place between heaven and hell, where one may have to wait for sins to be absolved before being admitted into heaven

RELIC A scrap of clothing, bone, or other artifact from the life of a saint, which is believed to help its holder in understanding the saints and scriptures and sometimes to have healing properties as well

RESURRECTION The rising of Jesus from death into new life

RITUAL A regular, repeated practice in church life

ROSARY A circular string of beads with a crucifix attached, used as a devotional aid in the practice of Catholicism

SABBATH A day of rest for Christians, usually Sunday

SACRAMENT One of five (for Protestants) or seven (for Catholics) formal rites of church life

Pulpit

SACRIFICE In Christianity, the act of giving something up or accepting hardship to benefit someone other than oneself

SACRISTY *see* VESTRY

SAINT A person whose good works on earth have earned him or her official recognition for holiness in the Christian church; sainthood is not conferred on people until after their death

SCHISM A formal division; specifically, one of two major breaks in the Christian Church: between the Eastern and Western church in the 11th century, and between two (and later three) popes during the 14th and 15th centuries

SCRIPTURE The writings of the Bible

Pietá

SECT *see* DENOMINATION

SHRINE A place or object of worship

SOUL The spiritual part of a person, as opposed to the corporeal body

SPIRE A vertical, pointed structure that rises above a church's main roofline

STOLE A long, thin band worn over the shoulders of a priest. It often reflects the colors of the church seasons.

TRANSUBSTANTIATION The transformation of bread and wine into the actual body and blood of Christ during the celebration of the Eucharist (as opposed to the belief that the bread and wine merely represent these substances)

TRINITY The three aspects of God, consisting of the Father, Son, and Holy Spirit

VESTMENTS Ceremonial clothing

Vestments

VESTRY A room, usually on the grounds of a church, used for church meetings

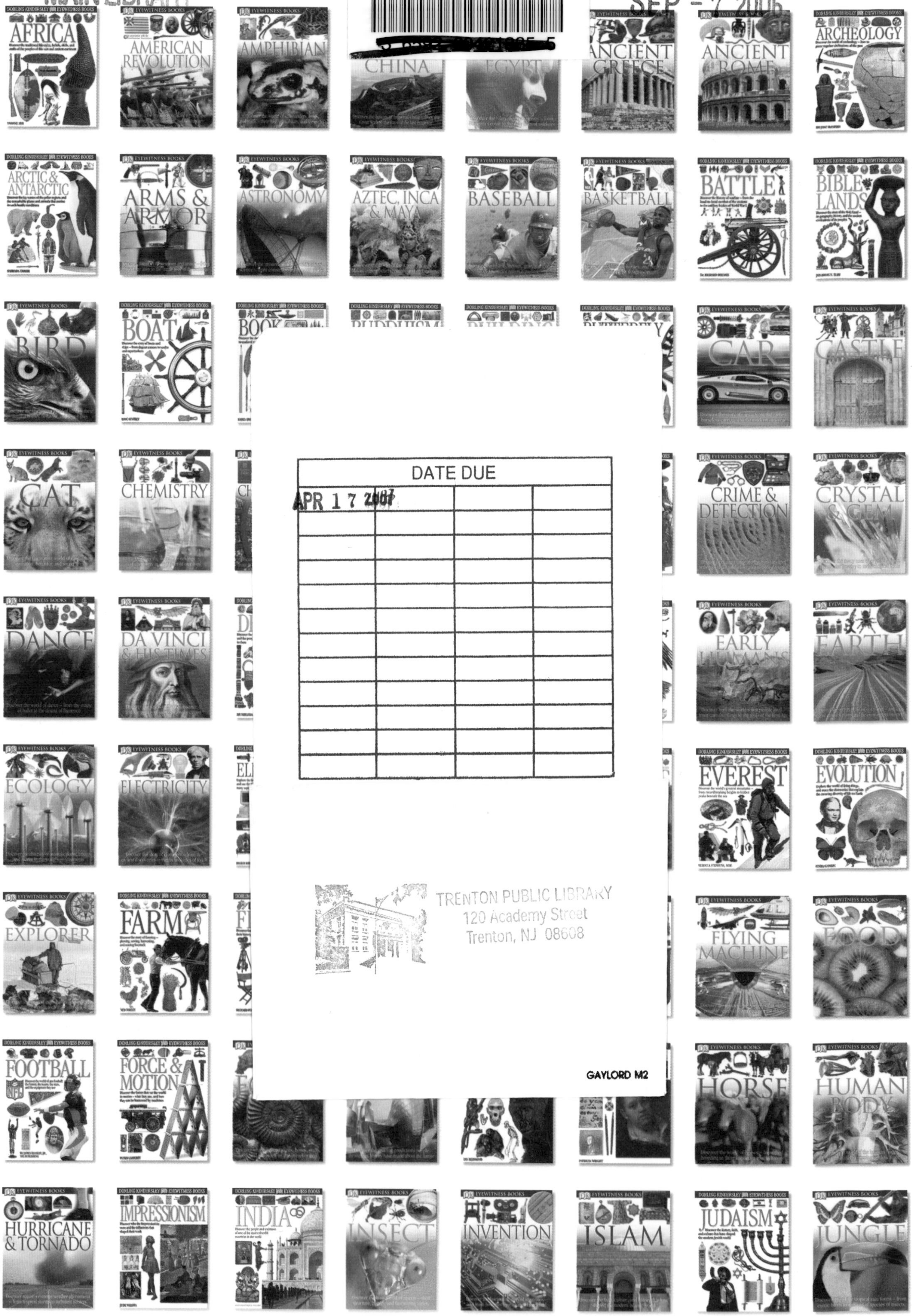

AFRICA

AMERICAN REVOLUTION

AMPHIBIAN

CHINA

EGYPT

ANCIENT GREECE

ANCIENT ROME

ARCHEOLOGY

ARCTIC & ANTARCTIC

ARMS & ARMOR

ASTRONOMY

AZTEC, INCA & MAYA

BASEBALL

BASKETBALL

BATTLE

BIBLE LANDS

BIRD

BOAT

BOOK

BUDDHISM

BUILDING

BUTTERFLY

CAR

CASTLE

CAT

CHEMISTRY

CRIME & DETECTION

CRYSTAL & GEM

DANCE

DA VINCI & HIS TIMES

EARLY HUMANS

EARTH

ECOLOGY

ELECTRICITY

ELE

EVEREST

EVOLUTION

EXPLORER

FARM

FLYING MACHINE

FOOD

FOOTBALL

FORCE & MOTION

HORSE

HUMAN BODY

HURRICANE & TORNADO

IMPRESSIONISM

INDIA

INSECT

INVENTION

ISLAM

JUDAISM

JUNGLE